WORSHIP
OR
FLEE

WORSHIP
OR
FLEE

31

DEVOTIONS SELECTED FROM

DANGEROUS GOD

Jim Albright

*Appreciation for **Dangerous God** on which these meditations **Worship or Flee** are based*

As you cannot judge a book by its cover, so in this case you cannot judge a book by its title. *Dangerous God* is actually a book of good news—terrifyingly good news—because it is a book full of truth about God. Admittedly, it is truth about God that is often overlooked, ignored, or even denied, but it is truth, nonetheless. It is also hard truth in the sense that instead of giving us "warm fuzzies," it causes cold shivers. But it is good truth in that it corrects the lopsided view of God that is common in contemporary Christianity. If you want to know God more as He reveals Himself in the Bible than as we think we want Him to be, you'll be grateful for this book.
DONALD S. WHITNEY: Professor of Biblical Spirituality and Associate Dean, The Southern Baptist Theological Seminary, Louisville, Kentucky; USA

Jim Albright balances our typically skewed view of God by showing us that he is not only merciful, but also wrathful. Euphemistic thinking about God is not truthful thinking about God. God, in fact, is more merciful than we have ever thought because His just judgment is more severe than we have ever thought. This book, as shocking as it might be, is a needed corrective.
JIM ELLIFF: President of Christian Communicators Worldwide and a founding pastor of Christ Fellowship of Kansas City, Missouri, USA

Jim Albright's latest book is an excellent summary of the often-forgotten doctrines of God's wrath and judgment. He calls believers to a serious reconsideration of our weak contemporary ideas of God as merely loving. This book provides a sobering call to the biblical reality of the wrath of God and an honest reminder of the consequences of ignoring the God who judges all.
JIM EHRHARD: Ph.D. of Theology, Professor at Kiev Theological Seminary, Kiev, Ukraine

Christianity in America has become very man-centered, resulting in the avoidance and neglect of God's wrath, vengeance, recompense, and terror. When I think deeply about a being who will condemn human

souls to an eternity of torment but also gladly sacrificed His only Son to a gruesome death to save human souls in rebellion against Him, I'm left in wonderment. Albright focuses on the attributes of God we naturally avoid but so desperately need if we are truly seeking the one, true, living God. As I read *Dangerous God*, the Lord's Spirit deflated my pride, exposed my man-centeredness, and rekindled my fear of the Lord to the praise of His glory and the joy of my soul.
BRAD VADEN: Pastor of Grace Baptist Church, Scott, Arkansas, USA

Albright's new book, *Dangerous God*, is not like any other book you will likely find in the twenty-first century. Albright dares to declare the true nature of the God who inhabits the universe. Many pastors and authors in our fearful-of-offending-others culture shy away from speaking about the true God of the Bible—a God of wrath, anger, and vengeance against sin and sinners. . .but Jim's book doesn't contain a single "shy" word in it. Jim's not interested in presenting a huggable God that the modern church can easily relate to, but the majestic God that is, the God in whose presence man should tremble. And he's convinced that getting to know this God, and not the domesticated God you've most likely been presented, is the best thing that can happen to you. To live a life in the fear and awe of the living God is truly to live a life worth living.
KEITH JONES: Missionary and Founding Pastor of Centro Veritas Church, Milan, Italy

We are quick to use the word "saved" when we refer to people coming to faith in Jesus. We often say, "We are saved from our sins." To somehow believe that we have been saved from something to do with us is a grave error. When through faith in Christ we are saved, we are saved from the wrath of Almighty God. Jim's book shows just what we are saved from and, on the flipside, what we are facing if we do not accept Jesus. This is a no-holds-barred exposé of the God no one wants to talk about because we have applied a "political correctness" filter to our twenty-first-century god that makes Him easier to accept. This book is written in love. It is one of the most honest books about the One True God. You owe it to yourself, your loved ones, and your neighbors to read it.
ALAN JOHNSTON: Ordained Minister in the Presbyterian Church of Ireland since 1998; Pastor of Killinchy Presbyterian Church

Worship or Flee
31 Devotions Selected from the Book *Dangerous God*

Jim Albright

Copyright © 2022 by Jim Albright

ISBN : 979-8-9864349-2-6

www.dangerousgod.com

Unless otherwise noted, Scripture quotations taken from the New American Standard Bible® (NASB), Copyright © 1960, 1962, 1963, 1968, 1971, 1972, 1973, 1975, 1977, 1995 by The Lockman Foundation. Used by permission. www.Lockman.org

Cover design and typeset by www.greatwriting.org
Cover design consultation: Jim Albright / James Holmes

Great Writing Publications
Taylors, SC
www.greatwriting.org

Table of Contents

Foreword..12

Preface 14

The God Who Is 16

Looking at All of Him 20

A Dangerous Oversight 24

Isaiah's Problem is Our Problem 28

There is No One Like You! 32

Lethal Holiness 36

One Sin..40

Rebellious Adjectives 44

There is None Who Seeks for God 48

God Rains Down Justice 52

A Good Judge...56

A Modest Salvo..60

God Is Not Mocked 64

God's Judicial Prerogative..68

That You May Know!...72

Darkness, Gloom, Fire and a Promise..............................76

God Is Unapologetic 80

Annihilation 84

Satan's Best Con 88

God Crushes Spiritual Infidelity: 1..................................92

God Crushes Spiritual Infidelity: 2 96

Hell—Infinite Outrage 100

Hell—The Lamb's Presence..104

Hell—Beyond Human Description 108

The Angry Lamb 112

The Atrophied Church 116

The Bottom-Line Question 120

Stunned, Staggered, Breathless Awe!..124

"Mary!"..128

Do You Really Believe?..132

A Thrilling Fear 136

About the Author..140

Worship the LORD
with reverence and rejoice with trembling.

Psalm 2:11 (NASB95)

Foreword

Why do you drink coffee in the morning? The taste is one reason. But the energy slap of caffeine is likely the main motive. You need that jolt in the morning to bring your body out of its nighttime sluggishness to full attention in order to get a good advantage on the day.

Worship or Flee is a way to get that requisite jolt every day for a month—an unforgettable month. Read it to start your day as you begin those cherished moments in your Bible and in prayer before God.

Devotional books are varied. Many of them are designed to calm you down, to offer something sweet to the taste, to comfort you before the difficult day. We need that. But we also need what author Jim Albright is pouring into our cup. It's for our soul.

Years ago, I developed a set of teachings on the fear of God. It was both salient and striking to me and, I believe, to many others. The sessions presented God as many had not known Him. The understanding of God that most believers have exhibits Him as too soft, too docile, and too comfy, yet the God of the Bible is both a tender Father and a powerful Potentate. As loving as He is, He is not to be trifled with.

The God who has had mercy on us through the sacrifice of His Son and surprises us with daily benefits, is also the One who has a raging righteous jealousy for His honor and brings a severe unbending judgment on His enemies. He has wrath, and He can do something about it. There is balance there, but on either side is the perfect extreme. We need a much truer understanding of who He is in *all* His glory.

The author invites you to know the truth about God. Thirty-one days of meditating on our "dangerous God" is an antidote to that one-sided portraiture of God we have concocted in our minds, which diminishes His true greatness and, even if unwitting, deprecates His character.

Drink all of it.

JIM ELLIFF:
President of Christian Communicators Worldwide
Kansas City, Missouri, USA

Preface

Worship or flee?

Really? That's the title of your devotional book?...

I know . . . it's not exactly what one might expect. No doubt the title has "put-off" more than a few. But surely—not the true lover of Jesus Christ. We've read our Bibles. We know what He says. We know what He's like. We not only understand the title's juxtaposition . . . we love it.

Yahweh is a full-disclosure God. He is wholly transparent in His Word. He is not one dimensional. In fact, He is infinitely complex. Yes, He has revealed Himself to be a God of inexpressible love and grace, but most assuredly, He has likewise disclosed that He will execute unspeakable wrath and vengeance upon His enemies. Inexcusably, the latter truth is one that much of the modern church has consciously decided to ignore.

This fact cannot be pleasing to the Almighty, for He has forthrightly commanded His people to behold *both* His kindness *and* severity. He has revealed exactly who He is for every intelligent being to behold and consider. He is unrepentant regarding His awful majesty and fearful greatness. It has always been "worship or flee" with Jehovah!

Please allow me a few brief excerpts from the closing chapter to whet your appetite for a devotional book that would dare to carry such a title.

The fear of God is the most beautiful, powerful, meaningful, fulfilling, and yes, exuberant place to live. If you call yourself a Christian and don't know this—you're doing it wrong.

We all must learn the one indispensable lesson of

this life—to tremble before our Creator with complete delight in abandoned worship. This happens only as we learn God fully . . . coming to fear Him as He has commanded.

For indeed, to genuinely fear the biblical God is to fear nothing else. To fear the biblical God is to be progressively liberated from every form of anxiety and slavery. To fear the biblical God is to find the breathtaking purpose for which our soul and mind were created—namely, ever-intensifying, awed intimacy with our Maker.

The proper fear of God—this stunned wonder and captivated reverence—fully animates the human spirit and intellect. To walk in perpetual amazement of Yahweh is to be truly alive! To learn to consciously abide in the never-ending, ever-increasing wonderment of Jesus Christ is to fully live.

I invite you to join this sojourn through the Scriptures. It's just simple obedience. The prophet has exhorted His people, "Behold your God!" (Isaiah 40:9).

1

The God Who Is

---

*"For I am God and there is no
other; I am God and there is
no one like Me . . ."*
Isaiah 46:9

God is probably not who you think He is. That is, if you're the average professing Christian, going to your average church. Sure, you have some concept of a supreme being—but is your god-notion, God? The one true God? The biblical God? The God who is?

To anyone who has ears to hear, I would simply like to say that it's time to open the Book and behold the breathtaking awe and terrifying holiness of Jehovah-God.

It's time to take what He says about Himself seriously, for El Shaddai will not countenance being pushed to the periphery of a trivial, religious parody. The biblical God is, by definition, the antithesis of peripheral. He *will* be central, for He *is* central whether your preacher and denomination like it or not.

It's time to know, believe, and delight in *all* that God has revealed about Himself. For indeed, to honestly look at the unredacted God of the Bible is to never be the same. And aren't you way past ready to go on with God?

If you have left off your pursuit of Him in His Word, I caution that this is a grievous error. You *must* go on with God! You *must* tremble afresh and anew! This is an ever-present necessity for every true believer.

To be sure, God is unrepentant. He is unapologetic regarding His awful majesty and fearful greatness. He has, quite literally, gone public with the infinite fury that is irrevocably grounded in His absolute holiness and abhorrence of sin. His anger is splashed all over the pages of Scripture. He has unashamedly revealed exactly who He is for every intelligent being to behold and consider.

If you do not know that the God of the Bible is a God of fierce wrath and horrifying vengeance, you have chosen willful ignorance. Such deception may afford you some superficial peace of mind just now, but worshiping and trusting your god-notion will ultimately cost you everything—forever.

For indeed, the God who is, the biblical God, has revealed Himself to be the most dangerous Being in the cosmos for all who would make themselves His enemy. This is the God who is. The you-cannot-see-My-face-and-live God of Scripture who strikes fear in the heart of every thinking human being.

We need this. We were made for this. We were wired for awe and wonder. The human soul longs for the transcendent, the eternal, the infinite—an awesome, fearsome, consuming-fire God. Yahweh is His name!

I simply can't get interested in the generic caricatures of God being dispensed in the media, in world religions, and yes, even in a pseudo-church near you. I desire to know the reigning God, the God of the Bible, before whom every thinking person reflexively trembles and the whole earth spontaneously shakes.

Only my Creator-Redeemer God, Jesus Christ, can fill the eternity He put into my thirsty heart. I must have Him . . . all of Him. He is the one non-negotiable for every awakened and alive soul. I cannot and will not settle for some domesticated iteration—some denominational pseudo-Christ. I can't live that small. I won't!

"A jealous and avenging God is the
LORD; The LORD is avenging and
wrathful. The LORD takes vengeance
on His adversaries, and He reserves
wrath for His enemies. . . . Who can
stand before His indignation?
Who can endure the burning
of His anger?"
Nahum 1:2, 6

2

Looking at All of Him

"Prepare to meet your God . . . ."
Amos 4:12

Every born-again lover of Jesus Christ effortlessly delights in and treasures His amiable attributes. Yes, He is a God of inexhaustible love, grace, mercy, patience, and benevolence. Every true believer fluently exults in the unfathomable kindness God has lavished upon us!

My poverty, and likely yours, is that I have not immersed myself in God's holiness, righteousness, and justice from which flow His wrath, vengeance, recompense, and terror in judgment. How is it possible that we should neglect this revealed dimension of God? We must not! It is a kind of backhanded blasphemy. This pursuit is necessary for you and me. We must comprehend Him more completely . . . more accurately.

If we do not give ourselves to this quest, our worship, and thus our lives, will unavoidably reflect a rather pedestrian view of our Creator. We simply will have no life-altering sense of His holy otherness, and consequently, His stunning condescension and work upon the Cross. Choosing not to pursue Him in all His fullness will ultimately diminish our understanding of who He *truly* is, and in due course, retard our faith, joy, thankfulness, repentance, humility, obedience, and zeal.

We must fear Him as He intends. We need to know Him like this. If we do not, it could rightly be said that we do not know Him at all. Considering His Self-Revelation in Scripture, this "not knowing" can only be characterized as wholesale neglect on our part. This carelessness will perpetually redound to our spiritual poverty. For indeed, it is proper that we would know, love, and feast upon *all* that God is.

We're all taught the right words—yes, He is an awesome and fearsome God! But knowing the words and genuinely "feeling" their heart-shaking reality deep within our souls are two dramatically different things. I'm talking about experiencing awe in such a way that it radically alters the way we think about everything. Yes, everything.

A biblically correct view of God must become our comprehensive, default premise in every circumstance of life. This is true whether we're talking about our marriage, our singleness, our life's work, our budget, or our Internet history. God, rightly viewed, alters every aspect of our lives.

It's a proper fear of the breathtaking, and yes, dangerous God who made us. Nothing is ever quite the same when you see Him as He has revealed Himself—a God of infinite wrath, vengeance, recompense, and terror. Once He has been seen in His fullness, the thoughtful person can never go back to business as usual. Never.

As I've persisted in reading the Bible over the last three and a half decades, I've continually encountered passage after passage bluntly pressing home these attributes. We must not only learn God *correctly*, we must also learn Him *fully*. It is the supreme discipline of every authentic disciple—to never stop looking at all of Him in all of His Word!

For God expects His people to both understand and, without hesitation, heartily echo the psalmist's cry of worship, "O Lord, God of vengeance; God of vengeance shine forth! Rise up, O Judge of the earth; render recompense to the proud" (Psalm 94:1-2). If this God, the God of the Bible, is in full view, men and angels have but two viable options—worship or flee! This is what God intends every one of His moral creatures to comprehend in the deepest core of their being.

"The sorrows of those who have bartered for another god will be multiplied . . . ."
Psalm 16:4

3

A Dangerous Oversight

*"Wail, for the day of
the LORD is near!"*
Isaiah 13:6

The nominal churchgoer doesn't quite understand the words of Isaiah quoted above. He likely attends a breezy-it's-mostly-all-about-you church. The words wrath, vengeance, recompense, and terror are never spoken in regard to his denominational god.

These biblical words are utterly alien to his concept of deity. His pseudo-Christ would never threaten wrath—he's too loving. His caricatured Jesus would never talk vengeance—he's too forgiving. His neutered god would never mention recompense. Seriously, what does that even mean to a respectable church member with the always-affable god of an utterly compromised Christianity?

To the nominal Christian, it is totally shocking and completely outrageous to infer that his cordial god would ever use the word terror in relation to anyone. How could that even be possible? The apathetic congregant has been repeatedly told by his minister, and that devotional book someone gave him some years ago, as well as what he's gleaned from the culture at large, that his god loves him and has a wonderful plan for his life. Obviously, his god is crazy about him! What else could he possibly need to know? Yes, eat, drink, hoard up a bunch of cash and retire well, for his god is an easygoing, compliant, and ultimately very useful deity.

What our lethargic Christian needs to know is what his preacher has not been telling him—that his lukewarm Christianity will take him to hell. He's the kind of professing Christian who will inevitably hear those cataclysmic words from the lips of Jesus Christ that his preacher never failed to omit from his sermon—"I never knew you, depart from Me . . . ." (Matthew 7:23).

American theologian Michael Horton is right, "Nobody today seems to think that God is dangerous. And that is itself a dangerous oversight." Amen! In brilliant fashion, *Desiring God* senior writer Tony Reinke adds that this ". . . is dangerous because before we yawn at God, we must first replace . . . and domesticate [Him] . . . . Who wants a God who roars, threatens, who judges? Why not rather fashion a god in our taste—a friendly god we can pet, leash, and export for popular appeal?"[1]

So, true believer, in this devotional journey, I call you to a profoundly deeper place with Jesus Christ, that you might know Him more fully and worship Him more completely. It is my prayer that you will learn to tremble with utter, perfect, complete humility, reverence, and joy at who He is.

And . . . that this more fully informed and felt awe will inevitably seep into every corner of your life. We must be changed afresh and anew as we learn to fear Him with perfect delight! For indeed, fear and gladness coexist in every regenerate heart!

And to the casual church attender, I exhort you to put down your pseudo-Christian god and your denominational affections and run to the God "who dwells in unapproachable light" for the salvation of your soul. Pseudo-Christianity will not save you from this justly incensed God. You must be reconciled to the God who is—the terrifyingly magnificent God of unsearchable greatness before whom the whole earth trembles and the mountains melt like wax.

1 Tony Reinke, "Stop Apologizing for God," Desiring God Website, October 25, 2014, accessed July 10, 2016, https://www.desiringgod.org/articles/stop-apologizing-for-god.

"Those who hate the LORD would
pretend obedience to Him; and their
time of punishment would be forever."
Psalm 81:15

4

Isaiah's Problem Is Our Problem

"Woe is me, for I am ruined"
Isaiah 6:5

Why Isaiah's impassioned lament here? Because God granted him an unencumbered glimpse of Himself.

And with that vision of the "King of glory" on His throne, Isaiah immediately knew two things were inescapably true—God is holy, and he was not. This is the real-life, calamitous condition of every human being. And this, if not remedied, will result in each one of us meeting God as an enemy.

Of course, Isaiah knew God was holy, at least intellectually. It was Jewish doctrine and history. But now, he has glimpsed God and his abstract notions of what holy meant have been obliterated. Instantaneously, God's holiness was a heart-quaking, fear, and trembling reality.

Other translations of the Bible put the words "undone, lost, doomed, and destroyed" in Isaiah's mouth. For the first time in his life, he had some genuine insight into the awesome God who is. And consequently, for the first time in his life, he had some small awareness of the horrific nature of his sin.

No more pleasant fictions about who he thought he was before Yahweh. No more divine misconceptions. No more religious delusions. Now, there was no doubt; he was hopelessly exposed. In an instant, his rather high opinion of himself was destroyed.

He experienced, as American theologian R. C. Sproul writes, "pure moral anguish, the kind that rips out the heart of a man and tears his soul to pieces . . . [as] relentless guilt screamed from his every pore."[2] Isaiah now knew without doubt that he was exhaustively ruined—from the inside out. This is what it's like for a human

2   R. C. Sproul, *The Holiness of God* (Carol Stream, IL: Tyndale Momentum, 1998), 30.

being to come face-to-face with Yahweh.

Isaiah's problem is, in fact, our most urgent and grave problem—God is holy and we're not. All our other problems pale in comparison. They are temporal and will all soon be six feet under with our corpse. The God-is-holy-and-we're-not problem will transcend our dignified funeral. Indeed, it will define every second of our eternity.

If you don't know that this is true, you've not yet genuinely encountered the biblical God. The God Isaiah saw. The God who reflexively evokes the word "woe" deep within the human soul. The God before whom, no one ever yawns.

The Bible records that every man granted a glimpse of the awesome, overpowering, yes, crushing holiness of God as Isaiah did, was similarly affected:

> Moses "hid his face, for he was afraid to look at God."
> Joshua "fell on his face to the earth."
> Ezekiel "fell on [his] face . . . ."
> Daniel's "color turned to a deathly pallor and [he] retained no strength . . . with [his]face to the ground."
> Peter, James, and John "fell on their faces and were much afraid."
> Paul "fell to the ground . . . ."
> And John again, in receiving the Revelation, "fell . . . as a dead man."

These are the instinctive, seemingly involuntary responses of God's prophets and apostles when confronted with His overwhelming supernatural, personal presence. Canadian pastor Tim Challies is spot on when he writes, "The basic human condition is to believe that God isn't really all that holy and that I'm not really that bad . . . . So we are a good match, God and I."[3] This is a miscalculation of infinite and everlasting proportions.

3   Tim Challies, "God's Not Really That Holy, I'm Not Really That Bad" Challies. com, November 9, 2015, accessed August 15, 2019, https://www.challies.com/articles/gods-not-really-that-holy-im-not-really-that-bad/

❖

*". . . For in Your sight no man
living is righteous."*
Psalm 143:2

5

There is No One Like You!

---

*"Holy, Holy, Holy
is the LORD of hosts . . . ."*
Isaiah 6:3

We truly need to understand just what is being said about God as the thrice-holy Sovereign of heaven and earth. What is this unique attribute of God from which wrath, vengeance, recompense, and terror lavishly flow?

The textbook definition of *holy* reveals several facets—it references deific power, magnificence, and, of course, purity. Lastly, there is the principal connotation that Isaiah is communicating to us—God's otherness.

God is set apart, distinct, separate, other, foreign. Of course, if He is God, He is, by definition, infinitely above, outside, and beyond His creation. The Scriptures reveal that the supernatural otherness of God evokes an impulsive terror in the heart of humanity. Again, R. C. Sproul writes . . .

> When we encounter Him, the totality of our creatureliness breaks upon us and shatters the myth that we have believed about ourselves, the myth that we are demigods, junior-grade deities who will try to live forever . . . God is too great for us; He is too awesome . . . . In His presence we quake and tremble. Meeting Him personally may be our greatest trauma.[4]

There is nothing more true in all creation than the fact that, apart from a saving relationship with Jesus Christ, meeting God *will be* our greatest trauma—an everlasting and infinite trauma!

Isaiah heard the seraphim call out to his colleague,

4 R. C. Sproul, *The Holiness of God* (Carol Stream, IL: Tyndale Momentum, 1998), 44.

"Holy, Holy, Holy, is the Lord of hosts. The whole earth is full of His glory." John heard a similar refrain from the four living creatures in the Revelation. "Holy, Holy, Holy, is the Lord God the Almighty, who was and who is and who is to come." In the Bible, no other attribute of God is used in this way—as a thrice-echoed appellation of worship from creature to Creator.

We do not see such worship built around any of God's other manifold characteristics. To borrow from Sproul again, there is no biblical chorus of "'love, love, love' or 'mercy, mercy, mercy' or 'wrath, wrath, wrath' or 'justice, justice, justice,'" recorded in God's Word. The hosts of heaven are letting us know what *the* transcendent attribute of God is; His holy-otherness. These captivated angelic beings are acknowledging and proclaiming what every creature viscerally knows: "There is no One like You! There is no One like You! There is no one like You!"

It can be no coincidence that after Isaiah's vision, he wrote some of the loftiest prose in all the Bible regarding the supernatural otherness of God. It is the unyielding chorus of Isaiah chapters 40 through 46 where God unapologetically states that He is God and nobody else is! Yes, the biblical God is other. He is the unrivaled Uncreated, the unequaled Unbegun. Of course, the thoughtful person must "worship or flee!"

"'To whom then will you liken Me, that
I would be his equal?'
says the Holy One."
Isaiah 40:25

6

Lethal Holiness

"You cannot see My face, for no man can see Me and live."
Exodus 33:20

So, who plays games with the you-cannot-see-My-face-and-live God quoted here? Who in their right mind would be high-handed before "I Am Who I Am," and what would be the just consequences of such insanity? God does not leave us guessing in this regard.

While it is rare that God's justice is immediately visible—as we will witness in the following four biblical accounts—it is always and finally inevitable. Holiness is toxic to the unholy. Every day it is lethal to defy holy God, and His response comes solely at His discretion. It may be immediate as we will see from the pages of Scripture. Or it may come to us at the end of a long, healthy, prosperous, pseudo-Christian life.

HOLINESS AND DERELICTION: They were priests, Aaron's sons. They knew what God expected. It wasn't difficult. You know, just have enough conviction to be competent. But Nadab and Abihu couldn't seem to be bothered. Inexplicably, they offered "strange fire before the LORD."

"And fire came out from the presence of the LORD . . . and they died before the LORD." Was this a divine overreaction? No! It was the presumptuous unholy behaving badly in the very presence of the provoked Holy! That can only ever end one way . . . like this!

HOLINESS AND DEFIANCE: Korah was the great-grandson of Levi. He and his mates decided to take on God's man, Moses. He defiantly challenged God's prophet. Then the LORD told Moses to have the congregation "get back from around the dwellings of Korah, Dathan and Abiram." Not a good sign.

The Bible records that, "the earth opened its mouth and swallowed them up" and that fire came forth from the LORD and consumed 250 co-conspirators. Some in the camp grumbled—so immediately, the wrath of God went forth and 14,700 more were slain. This is the prerogative of Holy-Other every minute of every day—to violently take out the defiant!

HOLINESS AND DISOBEDIENCE: God brought the exodus Jews into the Promised Land warning them that all the precious items captured were holy to the LORD. Achan decided he would simply ignore God's command and keep some booty for himself. The text tells us that "the anger of the LORD burned."

Joshua tells us that he and all of Israel took Achan and all that he had stolen and his sons, his daughters, his livestock, and all that belonged to him, and all Israel stoned them with stones and burned them with fire.

HOLINESS AND DUPLICITY: There was immense joy in the congregation as the people decided to hold "all things in common." Ananias and his wife Saphira agreed to do the same, but they were not truthful regarding the sale of their property.

Peter said, "You have not lied to men, but to God." Ananias and Saphira were struck down by God and died on the spot. It was a breathtaking exhibition of incited Holiness. Religious duplicity is always met with divine indignation.

The world is saturated with obstinate men "given fully" to live unholy lives under the gaze of the Holy. This is idiocy of the highest order. The holy justice that was immediately issued forth in the above accounts reveal ultimate reality. They shock us because we are not well versed in ultimate reality. That's on us, for God has faithfully revealed that the Holy is always fatal to the unholy.

"Who will not fear, O Lord, and glorify
Your name? For You alone are holy. . . ."
Revelation 15:4

7

One Sin

---

*"Cursed is the ground
because of you . . . ."*
Genesis 3:17

Why all this mayhem and calamity in the world? Why all this suffering? Why all this personal tragedy? Why all these natural disasters? Why all this sickness and deformity? Why murder? Why pornography? Why false religion? Why terrorists? Why all this brokenness and heartache? Why all these wars? Why all this death?

Because of one sin. Just one.

One sin brought down paradise. Just one. One sin subjected a two-trillion galaxy cosmos to corruption. I want you to feel the weight and catastrophic scope of that. It was one sin. With one sin, humanity declared its independence from God, unleashing the knowledge of evil, and consequently, the just wrath, vengeance, recompense, and terror of Yahweh.

Why is the world messed up? It's not because God is messed up; it's because we messed up. The Bible is clear, we sinned in Adam. I know, some don't like the doctrine of original sin. What always matters is not whether we like a biblical assertion or not, but whether has God said it. With one sin *we* let loose the horrors of evil justly incurring God's inevitable and righteous response.

We ate of the "tree of the knowledge of good and evil" and have "reaped the whirlwind" of unrestrained wickedness and, yes, God's omnipotent fury ever since. Why all the evil in the world? We set that in motion by turning our backs on God. We are a damned species living on a condemned planet that is "reserved for fire." One sin did that as we tasted evil, and the thrice-holy God responded with perfect justice. The God who is, hates sin and as His psalmist reminds us, ". . . has indignation every day."

Sin is not merely breaking a law and consequently being estranged from God. Sin is the creature's white-hot rebellion against his Creator. Sin is not an error. It is more akin to a frenzied insurgence. This antipathy between God and man is the consequence of man's shocking decision to rebel against a benevolent Sovereign. Make no mistake, every sin is profoundly personal. It's between us and an incensed God—every time.

Sin is the suicidal exchange of the glory of God for sugar-coated substitutes. Why does any thinking person do this? It's truly hard to figure. There is something mysteriously dark, gloomy, macabre, and sinister in the fallen, rebellious nature of man. He enthusiastically runs to soulish destruction.

This is the ultimate cosmic outrage—eschewing God and preferring someone or something over Him. It is a forsaking of God to pursue some temporal pleasure that can never satisfy. God's prophet likens this psychosis to drinking from a dry well.

Mankind has shown that he is willing to exchange his soul at "Vanity Fair" for just about anything. From success, to . . . family, comfort, fine houses, acclaim, positions, games, politics, fictitious news, sexual perversion, fashionable religion, etc., etc., etc., *ad nauseum*. It's a not-so-subtle "No Thank You!" to the One who designed, created, and made bountiful provision for us. It quite naturally raises the question—How did we ever get to this unbelievably stupid and self-destructive place?

"... they have forsaken Me, the
fountain of living waters, to hew for
themselves cisterns, broken cisterns
that can hold no water...."
Jeremiah 2:13

8

Rebellious Adjectives

"Indeed, has God said . . .?"
Genesis 3:1

They had everything! It was a utopian wonderland! There was only beauty, peace, well-being, prosperity, and unbridled expectation all day, every day. There was only one command. Not five, or three, or two . . . just one. God had aggressively stacked the deck in their favor. This was doable. How could we mess this up?

So, who was this serpent in the garden? Ezekiel tells us that this was the blameless, anointed cherub dwelling on the holy mountain of God, possessing the seal of perfection, wisdom, and beauty until unrighteousness was found in him and God cast him to the ground. This angelic being had said, "I will ascend to heaven, I will make myself like the Most High." Satan is his name.

We've all heard the question. Namely, if God is both good, and omnipotent, why is there evil? It's important to note that, according to the summation of the creation account in Genesis, evil is not a created thing. For "God saw all that He had made . . . was very good." The Scriptures clearly reveal that evil arose from the free will, moral choices of the good, but mutable creatures God created. First through Satan and the mutineer angels who followed him, and then, through man.

The creature, created good, chose to depart from goodness—enter evil. The Bible is unequivocal on this point. The responsibility for the presence of evil in the world lands solely at the feet of the creature. I've always liked the analogies that darkness is no thing, and cold is no thing, but are merely the absence of light and heat. It could be said that evil is no thing, but the absence of love for God within the heart of the creature.

It is the clear biblical assertion that evil arises and metastasizes within the creature. Considering this scriptural reality, it is indeed the height of narcissistic audacity for humanity to then in turn point the finger at God. Obviously, to say evil came *from* God is blasphemous. But to in turn say evil did not come *by* God is equally blasphemous. Evil has come *by* good but not *from* good.

If we are Bible believers, we understand and heartily acknowledge that God is the reigning, ruling Sovereign of heaven and earth. Nothing, including evil, is beyond His reach, authority, and control. God, while not the author of evil, obviously had good reasons for allowing evil to arise from His good creation—not least being the glory of His Son in the redemption of His people.

Satan came to Eve with his two fundamental lies. One—God is not good . . . He is holding out on you. And two—disobedience is better than God. We bought it. The rest is history. Regarding humanity's rebellion, C. S. Lewis writes . . .

> They wanted, as we say, to "call their souls their own." But that means to live a lie, for our souls are not, in fact, our own. They wanted some corner in the universe of which they could say to God, "This is our business, not yours." But there is no such corner. They wanted to be nouns, but they were, and eternally must be, mere adjectives.[5]

Adjectives wanting to be nouns! Yes, every human being's aspiration since that catastrophic moment in history!

---

5   C. S. Lewis, *A Year With C.S. Lewis* (New York, NY: HarperCollins Publishers, 2003), 361.

❖

*"... and ... she took from its fruit and
ate; and she gave also to her husband
... and he ate."*
Genesis 3:6

9

There is None Who Seeks for God

"... there is none who does good,
there is not even one ...."
Romans 3:12

The Genesis text tells us that after the fall, Adam and Eve began their earnest search for God. Hasn't every human being eagerly sought for God since that fateful day? It's not that we're not looking, it's just that God is so hard to find. Oh wait! That's not it. The apostle is unequivocal: "There is none who seeks for God!"

This is who humanity is. All we have to do is watch the six o'clock news, read a newspaper, surf the Internet, or listen to ourselves for a little while. It's what we do. Listen to the prophet: "The heart is more deceitful than all else and is desperately sick; who can understand it?"

So, let's dispense with the mythology we want God, that humanity is searching for God, but just can't find Him. We're hiding just like Adam . . . because we are Adam. We know we are naked. We know we are exposed. We know we have transgressed the Word of God.

And while some may acquiesce to a little religion on Sunday, the very last thing many genuinely want to do is encounter the biblical God. Mankind is exactly like our first father and mother, hiding in the proverbial bushes. Its why pseudo-churches are full of people—all hiding from God in the most inconspicuous place.

God said to Adam, "Where are you?" Even in our premeditated rebellion, God came for us. God initiates. God seeks, that He may save. Yes, His righteous judgment upon our wanton mutiny will ultimately bring down the whole cosmos, but there is also provision made for any and all who would repent and believe.

Adam's a lot like you and me. He's pretty sure none of

this is his fault. He believes he's a bit of a victim here. I mean, why the tree? Why the prohibition? Granted there was only one command but, you know, why the one? Yeah, and why free will? Couldn't God have built a more user-friendly cosmos?

And while we're on this, why this woman that *You* gave me? And as God enquired of Eve, come to find out, she was a victim too! From her perspective, all this unpleasantness was the serpent's fault. It's exceedingly profitable for us all to understand the precise origin of human victimhood. It was all about a devil and rebellion. If you think you're a victim, Satan has you right where he wants you.

God judged mankind, and the whole cosmos was subjected to futility and corruption. That's how unspeakably monstrous one sin is before God. All this disorder in the universe is not some flaw in the Creator or in His handiwork. It's evidence of our guilt before Him and His perfect judgment against us.

Why all this calamity, suffering, and death? It is the consequence of one sin, and it all prefigures eternal ruin. God's visible judgment in the natural realm is warning us about the reality and severity of His promised judgment in the supernatural realm—hell . . . the ultimate, eternal, and infinite calamity. You and I are not victims. We are malevolent rebels who have offended a holy, almighty, and dangerous God. No, you have not misunderstood; it is as bad as it could possibly be!

"Behold, I am against you . . .
I shall punish you according to the
results of your deeds. . . ."
Jeremiah 21:13-14

10

God Rains Down Justice

---

*"I will blot out man whom I
have created from the
face of the land."*
Genesis 6:7

Google tells me 150,000 plus people will die today. It's the "wages of sin." We've earned them. God created man to live. We knowingly chose death. We did that. And death is coming for each of us . . . very, very soon.

False teachers tell us that God will not judge humanity because He is constrained by His love. Well, the false teachers are refuted 150,000 plus times per day. God has judged. God is judging. And God will judge. This is not some isolated, obscure biblical truth. It is, in fact, a pervasive scriptural reality.

Yes, God is love but obviously, as God, His emotional life is infinitely complex. He is more than one thing. Just as you and I are. "God is love" but He is also "fierce wrath." If we are to have any intellectual integrity with His Word, we must affirm that all of God does all that God does—namely, God's justice is expressed in perfect symmetry with His mercy. His compassion is expressed in perfect symmetry with His vengeance. And His wrath is expressed in perfect symmetry with His love.

You may think you're too sophisticated to believe the biblical account about Noah, the ark, the animals, and the Flood . . . but according to Matthew 24:37-39, Jesus Christ believed it. God incarnate had firsthand knowledge of Noah, the ark, the animals, and the flood. He rendered that judgment. He decreed the torrent.

So, why? Why this global cataclysm? To parrot the last few devotionals: sin. God would save only eight human beings: Noah and his immediate family. Why Noah? Because Noah found favor (or "grace" as the NKJV renders it) in the eyes of the LORD. This is always the biblical pattern. It is the sovereign and initiating grace of God being worked out in the life of a sinner through whom God works His purposes.

And Moses writes . . .

> In the six hundredth year of Noah's life, in the second month, on the seventeenth day of the month, on the same day all the fountains of the great deep burst open, and the floodgates of the sky opened. And rain fell upon the earth for forty days and forty nights . . . . And the water prevailed more and more upon the earth, so that all the high mountains everywhere under the heavens were covered. . . . Thus He blotted out every living thing that was upon the land, from man to animals to creeping things and to birds of the sky. . . . (Genesis 7:11-24)

Did you notice the specificity regarding the date the flood began? Yes, this is not a "once upon a time" thing. This is a historical account—not a fairytale. It is interesting to note that there are more than three hundred flood legends throughout the world among widely dispersed people groups.

This was a worldwide phenomenon, for "all the high mountains everywhere under the heavens were covered." You can't legitimately hide from that scriptural assertion unless, of course, you're a brazen, out-of-the-closet biblical reductionist—you know, one who enthusiastically edits the Bible with unqualified abandon. You know who you are.

"A destruction is determined,
overflowing with righteousness."
Isaiah 10:22

11

A Good Judge

*"God is a righteous judge and a
God who has indignation
every day."*
Psalm 7:11

In continuing to consider the biblical account of the flood, we are all sadly aware that many so-called Christians don't "kick-in" with the Bible until after Genesis 11, or even later. Yeah, the Garden of Eden, Adam and Eve, Noah's ark, and the Tower of Babel are all just so—what's the word—"unsophisticated"; "unenlightened."

The Genesis skeptics believe that anyone with an IQ of 85 or above simply could not condescend to embrace such obvious "folklore." Of course, and again, we're either Bible believers or we're not. The true Christian doesn't stand in judgment over God's Word.

We don't presume to have the right to choose what to believe and what to mythologize. The true lover of God is never His editor. Surely, if God can't be trusted to get the first eleven chapters of the Bible right, why would any rational person believe the remaining 1,178 chapters?

Apart from Noah and his family and the creatures in the ark, Genesis tells us that, in this judicial act, God killed every man, woman, boy, and girl, as well as "all flesh in which is the breath of life." How many people were there on the planet? What was the body count? Scholarly estimates run anywhere from 250,000 to 1,000,000,000 plus. No one knows, and ultimately, it's an academic question.

Again, God gives life and God takes life. He is the Creator. This is His prerogative. There is an important lesson here for us. God does not put the life of man above His glory. When once His longsuffering patience has been exhausted, He will be glorified in executing perfect justice. He will show forth His righteous indignation. This, of course, is shocking to the nominally Christian and biblically illiterate—but this is the dangerous God who is.

We do need to stop and think deeply about this. God killed them all. This is perfect holiness provoked by premeditated, obstinate rebellion. Just what is the job of a good judge? Dispense justice. Only one thing—dispense justice. It's what God did in the flood. Some might object. But God is on record. He has clearly said that to sin is to die. And He alone decides when our wages are due. Yes, God killed 250,000 to 1,000,000,000 plus people in the Flood. Does that offend you? Why? The wages of sin is death. Yahweh says this is justice. Not a good idea to get into that debate with Holy-Other.

We must always remember: God is under no obligation to save anyone. He made everything under the sun. It's His intellectual property. He is the Potter; He can do whatever He wants with "the thing molded," particularly when His creatures are in abject rebellion against His reign and benevolence. We have no claim on God's forbearance and mercy. You and I need grace, the unmerited favor of a justly incensed Sovereign.

Remember, too, that God never offered the angels a savior. He simply gave them what their rebellion warranted—justice. He rendered a righteous verdict of condemnation. It's what a good judge should do. It's what He should do with you and me. So, don't play the fool. Don't critique God for the flood. It was divine justice. Period.

*"And the heavens declare His
righteousness, for God
Himself is judge."*
Psalm 50:6

12

A Modest Salvo

"Then the Lord *rained
on Sodom and Gomorrah
brimstone and fire . . . ."*
Genesis 19:24

Moses writes, "Now the LORD appeared to [Abraham] by the oaks of Mamre." Yahweh confided in His chosen patriarch regarding the exceedingly grave sin of Sodom and Gomorrah. And Abraham asked, "Will You indeed sweep away the righteous with the wicked?"

This is a noteworthy question. God hasn't mentioned anything about sweeping anyone away. Where does Abraham come up with such a notion? He was only nine generations removed from Noah. Everyone knew what the flood had been about. Abraham didn't formally have Romans 6:23 in his theological lexicon but he didn't need it. He knew what was going on in the cities of the valley. He knew God. He could do the math. He knew what this divine visit meant—wrath, vengeance, recompense, and terror!

God sent His angels in to get the righteous. They came to Lot, Abraham's nephew who lived in Sodom. Lot recognized them as messengers from God and offered them sanctuary in his home, for he knew the dangers of the city. The Genesis text reads that

> . . . the men of Sodom, surrounded the house, both young and old, all the people from every quarter; and they called to Lot. . . "Where are the men who came to you tonight? Bring them out to us that we may have relations with them."
> (Genesis 19:4-5)

Or, as the Living Bible paraphrase renders it, so that the men of the city could "rape them." Being wholly consumed with homosexual lust, the men of Sodom persisted. So, the angels struck their attackers with blindness to render them harmless. The angels told Lot that God's wrath was coming upon the city. "So, the men seized [Lot's] hand, and the hand of his wife and the hands of his daughters" and brought them out.

And the LORD rained down fire. How many died? Clearly, no one knows but God Himself. But we could safely estimate thousands to tens of thousands in the various cities of the valley. What will be the final body count of God's spent justice as He brings human history on this condemned planet to a close? Ultimately . . . it will be billions. The judgments of the flood, and Sodom and Gomorrah, are but a modest salvo in God's shock-and-awe assault on those who are in conscious rebellion against Him.

Only four were saved from the fire of heaven. Lot, his wife, and their two daughters. Every other man, woman, boy, and girl in the valley was killed. Even Lot's wife eventually perished as she longingly looked back to Sodom during the conflagration. Jesus used her death as a warning to those who would set their hearts upon a world under the just condemnation of an incensed Creator. Christ said, "Remember Lot's wife. Whoever seeks to keep his life shall lose it, and whoever loses his life shall preserve it."

Ultimately, the Lord is saying you must let go of death to seize life. And, oh, by the way, He says, "I am the life." The born-again soul understands . . . there is a death to be had before we can ever really learn to live. As Jesus said many different times, in many different ways, this is, in the end, about the supreme affection of our hearts. Lot's wife loved this world. She refused to die to death, and she perished.

"Hear, O earth: behold, I am
bringing disaster. . . ."
Jeremiah 6:19

13

God Is Not Mocked

". . . for whatever a man sows,
this he will also reap . . ."
Galatians 6:7

If a farmer plants corn in the spring, he doesn't have to wonder what he will be harvesting come summer. So, too, in the spiritual realm. Job says, "According to what I have seen, those who plow iniquity and those who sow trouble harvest it."

In the street vernacular, we all understand—what goes around, comes around. This is indispensable wisdom, for indeed, Yahweh is never mocked. Or, as the Message Bible paraphrases, "No one makes a fool of God." In his self-absorbed arrogance, Pharaoh ordered the murder of every firstborn son of Israel. This would come back to him, his progeny, and his nation in the unrelenting, righteous, and terrible judgment of God.

Pharaoh's murderous edict is how Moses got in that wicker basket floating in the Nile. It's why he ended up being adopted by Pharaoh's daughter. It's how he got his name. It's why he was raised as a prince of Egypt becoming a "man of power in words and deeds." However, the Bible tells us that

> By faith Moses when he had grown up, refused to be called the son of Pharaoh's daughter; choosing rather to endure ill-treatment with the people of God, than to enjoy the passing pleasures of sin; considering the reproach of Christ greater riches than the treasures of Egypt; for he was looking to the reward.
> (Hebrews 11:24-26)

Yes, it's the reaping and sowing thing. It's true, as John

MacArthur preaches, "From a worldly perspective, Moses was sacrificing everything for nothing, but from a spiritual perspective, he was sacrificing nothing for everything."[6] Moses wisely decided that sowing into eternity made far more sense than sowing into this temporal life.

Moses faced the same decision each one of us faces. To align ourselves with the wealth, power, prestige, comfort, security, pleasure, and luxury of this world, or to align ourselves with God and His invincible purposes. Each of us must weigh it out.

The question always is—Do you hear gain in going with God? Or do you hear loss? Jesus says you must choose Him or the world. You cannot legitimately love both, for either you "will hate the one and love the other, or [you] will hold to one and despise the other."

God says it's your call. Where is gain for you? What do you desire? What do you want? What, or who, do you love preeminently? What are you seeking? Are you sowing into this life, or the next? Are you sowing death or life? For truly, it is a God-ordained verity, you will eternally reap whatever you temporally sow. Stop and think about that for sixty seconds.

6   John MacArthur, Sermon, Grace Community Church, Los Angeles, CA.

"So, they shall eat of the fruit of their
own way and be satiated with
their own devices."
Proverbs 1:31

14

God's Judicial Prerogative

*". . . I will set My eyes against
them for evil . . . ."*
Amos 9:4

The book of Exodus tells us that God called Moses to be His instrument in delivering Israel out of Egyptian bondage. Moses asked God His name. His response was, "I AM WHO I AM." Our Creator is the eternal-self-existent-transcendent-Other. Simply, the One who has always been and always will be.

As some preacher somewhere said, "God didn't say I AM whoever you want Me to be as long as you're sincere about it."—a pointed indictment upon much of what is called the modern Christian church. Pseudo-Christs abound. Apostate denominations will preach any christ, just any old christ, but never the biblical One. The false church is unwilling to proclaim the angry Lamb of Revelation 6 who is coming in great wrath.

The text tells us that Moses tried to excuse himself from God's call no fewer than five times. Considering that he was having a supernatural encounter with the Almighty One, his excuses were pretty lame. Yes, just like your excuses and mine when God calls us out of our comfort zones. Moses was making the same mistake we all tend to make when God calls us to go with Him. He was looking at his own resume and not God's. The latter of course, renders the former inconsequential.

Earlier in the exchange, God had asked Moses what he had in his hand. It was his staff. Essentially, God was saying, "I'll bring miracles and deliverance through your staff; all you really have to do is show up." It's what God always requires of those who profess to be His—show up, believing! It's always our very best worship and our most effective evangelism!

God tells Moses that He will harden Pharaoh's heart so that he will not let Israel go. God is not mocked! Whatever a man sows, he will most certainly reap. God is always doing two things in the world. Every day He is doing these two things. He is always saving, and He is always judging. As God delivers Israel, He is judging Egypt.

Pharaoh is resting comfortably in his luxurious palace, completely unaware that he has been irrevocably judged by his Creator. Nothing has changed outwardly, but it is all over inwardly. God has given Pharaoh over to the just consequences of his own willful rebellion. He's still walking around, living his "good life," but Pharaoh's sentence has been rendered. He is irreversibly damned. He is irretrievably destined to spend an eternity in hell. Naturally, this judicial prerogative of God gives every thinking person serious pause.

Indeed, the gavel has fallen in the courtroom of God. Pharaoh is guilty. Judgment has been pronounced. God will judicially harden Pharaoh's heart even as Pharaoh continues to harden his heart against God. Surely, as is always biblically true, God is sovereign, and man is responsible. Truly, the God who is, rules and reigns and manages His cosmos, as well as the lives of men, according to His dictates—not ours.

God repeatedly reveals that it is a dangerous dance to presume upon His patience and forbearance. It's the chilling chorus of Romans 1 as the Holy Spirit recounts the judicial decrees of God in giving mankind over to their lusts, their degrading passions, and their depraved minds. It's all over for Pharaoh. His eternal fate is divinely sealed. Only narcissistic fools play games with Jehovah.

"You, even You, are to be feared; And
who may stand in Your presence
when once You are angry?"
Psalm 76:7

15

That You May Know!

"Thus says the LORD. . . Behold,
I will kill your son. . . ."
Exodus 4:22-23

God says to Pharaoh, "For this very purpose I raised you up, to demonstrate My power in you, and that My name might be proclaimed throughout the whole earth." Egypt's destruction is historical evidence of the glory of God revealed in His infinite fury and power through the just devastation of His enemies. God repeatedly says that in His wrath, vengeance, recompense, and terror, *all* will "know that [He is] the LORD!"

I will not recount the plagues God unleashed upon Egypt, but it would be profitable for you to study them yourself for at least two reasons. One, they reveal a sobering truth about God. And two, they reveal a sobering truth about man.

First, the narrative underscores how competent and thorough God is in His judgments. When provoked to it, He is comprehensive, exacting, and exhaustive in His righteous recompense. He will be neither distracted nor dissuaded in crushing His enemies.

Secondly, the plague accounts highlight man's absolute and suicidal bent against his Creator, no matter how blatantly obvious the evidences of God's presence, power, and glory are. We need to learn and never forget that—God was relentless in His wrath poured out upon Egypt as He will be against every person who chooses to remain His adversary. We also need to learn and never forget that—Pharaoh was relentless in his obstinance toward God as are all men who love their sin more than their Creator.

In your study of God's judgments upon Egypt, note His rigor—He painstakingly destroys His enemy. Also, note

Pharaoh's tenacity—He is utterly unyielding in his rebellion against God. Yes, right here, in the judgment of Egypt, the truth about God and the truth about man played out.

In effect, God says this is personal. Again, sin always is with God. He says, "*I will kill* all the first-born of Egypt." This is God's divine right. He gives life and He takes life. This is His business. He renders our sin-wages, our recompense, to us as seems good to Him.

Obviously, we don't know how many died in the final plague. I've seen estimates of 20,000 to 100,000 plus. Again, the numbers are academic. The underlying reality is that the God who is, the biblical God, will execute His perfect justice in accordance with His unimpeachable purposes and based solely upon His flawless timetable. In this, Yahweh does not consult men or seek their sanction.

Indeed, the LORD will compel Pharaoh to concede that He is God! In the utter destruction of his nation, the Egyptian king will ultimately have no choice but to acknowledge that Yahweh is God. Truly, it will be the ever-present realization that will utterly overwhelm and grip his mind for a billion eternities in hell.

Finally, every human being will acknowledge that the LORD is God. Every knee will bow, and every tongue will confess that Jesus Christ is Lord to the glory of God the Father. Even the damned. In experiencing God's wrath poured out against him, Pharaoh finally believed that the LORD is God. Truly, he will never stop believing it, for there are no unbelievers in hell.

"Now the LORD said . . . for I have hardened [Pharaoh's] heart . . . that I may show these signs of Mine . . . that you may know that I am the LORD."
Exodus 10:1-2 (NJKV)

16

Darkness, Gloom, Fire and a Promise

"And . . . Moses said, 'I am full of fear and trembling.'"
Hebrews 12:21

The Genesis text tells us that in a night of "terror and great darkness" God made a covenant with Abraham. Likewise, Moses experienced much the same as he encountered Yahweh. . .He writes

> . . . there were thunder and lightning flashes and a thick cloud and a very loud trumpet sound so that all the people who were in the camp trembled . . . Mount Sinai was all in smoke because the Lord descended upon it in fire. . . and the mountain quaked violently . . . Moses spoke and God answered with thunder . . . . And when the people saw it, they trembled . . . . [And] said to Moses "Speak to us yourself . . . but let not God speak to us, lest we die."
> (Exodus 19:16, 18-19, 20:18-19)

The parallel account in the book of Hebrews records that Sinai was. . .

> a blazing fire, and . . . darkness and gloom and whirlwind. . . and the sound of words which sound was such that those who heard begged that no further word should be spoken to them. . . .
> (Hebrews 12:18-20)

Jehovah is awesome. He is fearsome. He is dreadful. He is frightening. This is all true because He is holy-other. He provokes fear, trembling, and terror in the heart of fallen man, even when encountered in His veiled glory. It's the natural confronted by the Supernatural. This is the unanimous and universal testimony of Scripture.

Isaiah's words are true—in the holy presence of God, humanity is instinctively inclined to hide ". . . from the terror of the LORD and from the splendor of His majesty." If the god you worship is not like this, you urgently need to know that your god is not God.

Now, back to Abraham's night of terror and darkness. . . God told His patriarch that the Hebrews would not return to the land until the fourth generation because "the iniquity of the Amorites is not yet complete." What is God saying about the Amorites (Canaanites) and their sin?

That they are in the midst of a Romans 1 judgment. God has exercised His judicial privilege. He has given the Amorites over to their lusts and degrading passions. It's the reprobate mind. Judgment is set and God's timing will be perfect. God said that these peoples had engaged in "every abominable act which the LORD hates . . . for they even burn their sons and daughters in the fire to their gods."

This was wholesale, complete, and perfect revolution against the God who is and against His moral boundaries. They denied themselves no self-indulgence. It was comprehensive debauchery. They wantonly gave themselves to "every abominable act" God loathes.

The inhabitants of Canaan were not cognizant of the fact that their sins were being vigilantly tallied and logged. They didn't know the precise moment when they would commit their last act of rebellion against their Creator . . . that very last deed of willful and haughty arrogance before God . . . that very last sin. But God did.

The die was cast. God would deliver Israel at just the right time to, in turn, use them as His vehicle of judgment upon the degenerate peoples of Canaan. Justice for every single, high-handed sin against God had been inviolably decreed and would come to pass. Recompense was coming and would be delivered through the business end of a Jewish sword.

"The LORD determined to destroy. . . ."
Lamentations 2:8

17

God Is Unapologetic

*". . . The LORD will swallow
them up in His wrath . . . ."*
Psalm 21:9

As God is leading Israel toward the Promised Land, He tells them that they "shall utterly destroy" the inhabitants of Canaan. Concerning the cities of the land, God says, ". . . you shall not leave anything alive that breathes." Israel will be the instrument of God's wrath, vengeance, recompense, and terror in Canaan. God has set His face against His adversaries.

Inexplicably, there was trouble in the Exodus. Israel had seen the jaw-dropping presence and power of God in their deliverance. Yet, they decided that what they really needed to do was worship a golden calf. On its face, this sequence of events is beyond comprehension. The biblical text tells us that as God's anger burned, so did the anger of Moses. About 3,000 men fell in God's judgment.

Later, as Israel is poised to cross the Jordan, they decided it might be a good idea to play religion with a local idol. The text reads that

> the LORD was angry against Israel. And the LORD said to Moses, "Take all the leaders of the people and execute them in broad daylight . . . so that the fierce anger of the LORD may turn away from Israel."
> (Numbers 25:3-4)

In addition to the commanded execution, God sent a plague among the people and 24,000 more died. You don't get to play fast and loose with I AM. Ever. You don't get to presume on His forbearance. Ever. You don't get to play religion in apostate denominations with their pseudo-christs. Ever.

As we have already seen in our very abbreviated review of Scripture thus far, sometimes God is longsuffering. Sometimes He is not. Premeditated, habitual, lifestyle sin against God, garnished with a little pseudo-Christianity, is like a perpetual game of Russian Roulette. Sooner or later, with sudden finality, you die—forever.

And God told Moses, "Take full vengeance for the sons of Israel on the Midianites," for they had enticed and facilitated Israel's idolatry at Shittim. In the action, the army of Israel killed every Midianite male but spared the women and children. The text reads:

> And Moses was angry . . . and said to them "Have you spared all the women? . . . Now therefore kill every male among the little ones, and kill every woman who has known man intimately. But all the girls who have not known man intimately, spare for yourselves. . . ."
> (Numbers 31:14-15, 17-18)

I know some proper church members are offended at such a directive. God is unapologetic. You don't have to like it. God doesn't care if you like it or not. He is not seeking your approval or mine. God did it. He is the final arbiter in all matters concerning sin and judgment. That is simply enough said for the born-again lover of God.

True believers never dare critique infinite Mind and His holy acts with our two-and-a-half pounds of fallen, sinful, carnal, temporal, finite gray matter. The genuine Christian is always willing to tremble before God, but never, never, never call Him to account for His actions. Remember that whenever you find yourself recoiling at God's ways in judgment, you must never forget two simple things. He is always right. And you are always wrong.

"... and they will have no ... survivors
from the calamity that I am going
to bring on them."
Jeremiah 42:17

18
Annihilation

"Behold, I am against you..."
Jeremiah 21:13

This is what God did in judging the Canaanite peoples. This is how He talks about it.

Concerning the two kingdoms east of the Jordan river, Moses writes . . . "So, we . . . utterly destroyed the men, women and children of every city. We left no survivors . . . and we smote them until no survivor was left" (Deuteronomy 2:34, 3:3).

Regarding Jericho, Joshua writes, "[We] utterly destroyed everything in the city both man and woman, young and old, ox and sheep and donkey, with the edge of the sword" (Joshua 6:21).

Following are some paraphrased and condensed excerpts of God's judgment of the Amorite coalition found in Joshua 10.

- The LORD confounded the Amorites and slew them with a great slaughter.
- Israel slayed them with a very great slaughter.
- Israel put the Amorite kings to death.
- In the city of Makkedah every person in it was utterly destroyed.
- The city of Libnah was struck, there were no survivors.
- Every person in the city of Lachish was struck by the edge of the sword.
- The King of Gezer came out against Israel. There were no survivors.
- Every person in the city of Eglon was struck with the edge of the sword.

- There were no survivors in the city of Hebron.
- The city of Debir was utterly destroyed. There were no survivors.

Regarding Canaan, the Bible records that Joshua left no survivors, utterly destroying all who breathed. The prophet tells us that "it was of the LORD to harden their hearts, to meet Israel in battle in order that He might utterly destroy them, that they might receive no mercy, but that He might destroy them" (Joshua 11:20).

It's one of the indisputable lessons of the Bible—when once God is provoked to destruction, He is proficient.

Regarding the first six books of the Bible, I once heard a dignified church member say something to the effect that his god "would never command the killing of women and children." I suspect there are millions of people who profess to be Christians who would heartily concur with such a sentiment.

Once again, we're either Bible believers or we're not. But if you're this guy, I would caution you in the strongest possible terms that you are worshipping an emasculated, counterfeit, sub-biblical, pseudo-god. Your god is not God. He is not the God of the Bible. He is not the dangerous God who inhabits the cosmos.

And those who consciously choose to worship a pseudo-christ will learn, firsthand, that God is meticulously faithful regarding His threatenings. Lest each one of us bows to the terrifyingly magnificent God of the Bible—the One who kills men, women, boys, and girls in accordance with His righteous judgements—we will most assuredly be storing up wrath, vengeance, recompense, and terror.

"Your ways and your deeds have
brought these things to you.
This is your evil. . . ."
Jeremiah 4:18

19

Satan's Best Con

---

*"You believe that God is one.
You do well, the demons
also believe. . . ."*
James 2:19

God hates mere religion. He always has.

Jesus Christ didn't mince His words. He pronounced damnation upon the religious leaders of His day, saying . . .

> Woe, woe, woe to you . . . for you are like whitewashed tombs . . . even so you too outwardly appear righteous to men, but inwardly you are full of hypocrisy and lawlessness . . . how shall you escape the sentence of hell? (Matthew 23:13-33)

Religion is Satan's best con. He's the "father of lies." And his religious fictions are taking billions to hell. It's the ultimate demonic scam. This of course includes the many and varied forms of pseudo-Christianity with its caricatured-christs—no doubt, the adversary's proudest achievement!

Affinity for me-centered religion is a pristine reflection of mankind's depraved heart. Man has always preferred a self-righteous, user-friendly, feel-good formula that can be employed to manage a custom-made deity. Domesticated gods are just so much more expedient. Denominational banality and rote ecclesiastical performance are simply a lot less bothersome than true repentance and unconditional obedience—the explicit call of the Son of God to anyone who would claim Him as Lord and Savior.

This fondness to leave the revealed truth and power of the biblical God for a low-stress, comfortable religious habit is graphically depicted in both Testaments.

There are numerous places to authenticate this reality in the Old Testament. Isaiah says it as well as any . . .

> For this is a rebellious people, false sons, sons who refuse to listen to the instruction of the LORD; Who say . . . to the prophets, "You must not prophesy to us what is right, speak to us pleasant words, prophesy illusions."
> (Isaiah 30:9-10)

The apostle warned of the same heretical drift in the New Testament—something that is a full-blown epidemic in what is called the church today. Paul writes . . .

> For the time will come when they will not endure sound doctrine; but wanting to have their ears tickled, they will accumulate for themselves teachers in accordance to their own desires; and will turn away their ears from the truth, and will turn aside to myths.
> (2 Timothy 4:3-4)

Pleasant words, illusions, unsound doctrine, and ear-tickling-teachers propagating myths—sounds like your average so-called Christian church almost anywhere in the world right now. Obviously, this is a can't-miss-church-growth strategy! A lot of people like church just fine as long as an emasculated god is served up.

Old Testament Israel preferred an edited god and employed their prophets for hire to lead the way. Jeremiah gives us God's assessment of these leaders and the calamitous consequences for the Jewish nation . . .

> The prophets prophesy falsely . . . . And My people love it so! . . . They have refused to repent . . . "Shall I not punish these people," declares the LORD . . . shall I not avenge Myself? . . . I will stretch out My hand against the inhabitants of the land. . . ."
> (Jeremiah 5:3, 9, 31, 6:12)

"'Do you not fear Me?' declares the
LORD. 'Do you not tremble
in My presence?'"
Jeremiah 5:22

20

God Crushes Spiritual Infidelity: 1

"For a spirit of harlotry is within them and they do not know the Lord."
Hosea 5:4

God's graphic pronouncements of judgment through His Old Testament prophets on a people who claimed to be His reveals everything we need to know concerning how He must view much of what is called the modern church.

Ultimately, the words of the Jewish prophets are Yahweh's message of judgment to any and all who would arrogantly disregard Him—*particularly* those who are guilty of feigning allegiance to Him. Truly, it's an exceedingly dangerous thing to sit in a church with no real intention of worshiping, loving, and obeying the God of the Bible!

Yahweh is not unclear about mere religious performance—He loathes it! Israel's prophets leave no doubt concerning those who are, at heart, indifferent toward the LORD—yes, there will be much wrath, vengeance, recompense, and terror. This is an indispensable lesson for every one of us to hear, understand, and take to heart. The dangerous God who is, does not tolerate spiritual infidelity— He crushes it!

If you have not read the prophets lately, I invite you to. It is extraordinarily valuable to read them at a slower-than-normal pace. It is immensely profitable to linger over words, phrases, and verses—to fully take each one into your heart and mind . . . to feel the weight of them. In thoughtfully considering the awful vengeance of God in the physical realm, we will, in turn, get some small sense of just how monstrous our lukewarm religion is in the spiritual realm.

In His many and varied judgments, God is telling us something about ourselves and our moral rebellion. God's spent wrath is, to borrow from John Piper, a "wake-up call, telling us that sin leads to things like this! God means for us to awaken from our dreamworld of thinking our sin is no big deal. It's a horrifically big deal."[7]

Following are some excerpts from a few of God's prophets to a people, mind you, who claimed to be His:

- "Woe to them, they have strayed from Me! Destruction is theirs . . . ." (Hosea 7:13)
- "The end has come for My people Israel. I will spare them no longer." (Amos 8:2)
- "Then they will cry out to the LORD, but He will not answer them. Instead, He will hide His face from them [and] execute vengeance, in anger and wrath..." (Micah 3:4, 5:15)
- ". . . And I will punish the men who are stagnate in spirit . . . ." (Zephaniah 1:12)
- "And they made their hearts like flint so that they could not hear . . . the words which the LORD of hosts had sent by His Spirit. . . ." (Zechariah 7:12)
- "'. . . just as He called and they would not listen, so they called and I would not listen,' says the LORD of hosts. . . ." (Zechariah 7:13)
- ". . . Woe to them! For they have brought evil upon themselves. . . . For they have. . . despised the word of the Holy One. . . . On this account the anger of the LORD has burned against His people. . . ." (Isaiah 3:9, 5:24-25)
- "According to their deeds so He will repay, wrath to His adversaries, recompense to His enemies. For the day of vengeance was in My heart. . . ." (Isaiah 59:18, 63:4)

To be continued. . . in the next reading.

---

7   John Piper, Sermon, Bethlehem Baptist Church, Minneapolis, MN.

*"This people honors Me with their lips,
but their heart is far away from Me.
But in vain do they worship Me. . . ."*
Matthew 15:8-9

21

God Crushes Spiritual Infidelity: 2

". . . And they have played the harlot, departing from their God."
Hosea 4:12

More of God's words of judgment are spoken against those who claimed to worship Him:

- "I am against you. . . My eye shall have no pity and I will not spare." (Ezekiel 5:8, 11)
- "All hands will hang limp and all knees will become like water. . . and though they cry in My ear. . . yet I will not listen to them." (Ezekiel 7:17, 8:18)
- "Utterly slay old men, young men, maidens, little children, and women. . . My eye will have no pity." (Ezekiel 9:6, 10)
- "I shall not relent, and I shall not be sorry. . . . I shall bring terrors on you. . . ." (Ezekiel 24:14, 26:21)
- "Have you not done this to yourself by. . . forsaking the LORD your God?" (Jeremiah 2:17)
- "They refuse to know Me. . . . I will not show pity. . . nor have compassion that I should not destroy them." (Jeremiah 9:6, 13:14)
- ". . . for I shall pour out their own wickedness on them. . . . For a fire has been kindled in My anger, it will burn upon you. . . which will burn forever." (Jeremiah 14:16, 15:14, 17:4)
- ". . . Thus says the LORD, 'Behold, I am fashioning calamity against you. . . .'" (Jeremiah 18:11)
- "And I Myself shall war against you. . . even in anger and wrath and great indignation." (Jeremiah 21:5)

So, what's left to say?

One sure deduction would be that if you still don't believe the biblical God is a God of great wrath, vengeance, recompense, and terror—you either have an acute learning impairment, or you simply prefer to delude yourself.

Thankfully, Yahweh is a full-disclosure God. We're not left to grope for truth in a vacuum. He has spoken. The Bible is clear. He is a magnificent Savior and, yes, He is a fearsome Judge. Again, He will be glorified as both. And, just a reminder, God is not seeking our approval regarding who He is and how He metes out the "wages of sin" in judgment. God is simply revealing Himself to any and all who will hear.

The God who is, blesses. And He ruins. He gives, and, in judgment, takes away. He brings eternal joy, and, by judicial decree, infinite terror. Hear His prescient words to the Exodus Jews regarding their eventual rebellion against Him. This passage clearly reveals His proficiency as both a benevolent provider and an indignant judge. God says through His prophet. . . .

> And it shall come about that as the LORD delighted over you to prosper you, and multiply you, so the LORD will delight over you to make you perish and destroy you. . . .
> (Deuteronomy 28:63)

Yes, God gives life, and He kills. He is pure delight and comprehensive horror. He is faithful to His word concerning both. This is always the Potter's right as He is pleased to display His glory in both His kindness and severity. And to any remaining critics of Jehovah regarding His holy justice employed against mankind's rebellion, I will simply quote His prophet: "Why should any living mortal, or any man, offer complaint in view of his sin?" (Lamentations 3:39).

"You have slain them in the
day of Your anger, You have
slaughtered, not sparing."
Lamentations 2:21

"You have slain them in the
day of Your anger, You have
slaughtered, not sparing."
Lamentations 2:21

22

Hell—Infinite Outrage

*". . . fear the One who. . . has
authority to cast you into hell;
yes, I tell you, fear Him!"*
Luke 12:5

I remind you that God's judicial verdicts in time are merely inaugural. His fierce adjudications upon the earth are only the beginning of an unending, omnipotent cascade of divine fury. More wrath is coming. Infinitely more. Everlastingly more.

We must seek to let our mind's eye adjust to a kind of timeless farsightedness, or you will never begin to feel the weight of the Son of Man's words regarding eternal judgment. We're all living on the edge of eternity. Forever is but one heartbeat away. Suffice to say, understanding Messiah's teaching here matters far more than anything else you've got going on right now.

The Bible vividly reveals that the horror of temporal judgment is but a faint glimmer of that which is to come—namely, divine indignation beyond the grave. God's eternal fury is without end. God's wrath, like Himself, is infinite. It is everlasting. After a billion eternities, God's anger will have only just begun to be poured out.

God means for you to understand that this is a fixed reality in the cosmos. This is not religious myth or ecclesiastical bluff. Infinite outrage awaits every unrepentant soul. Provoked holiness knows no bounds. Renown, eighteenth-century American theologian, Jonathan Edwards, gives us some perspective here. Regarding the occupant of hell, he writes. . .

It would be dreadful to suffer this "fierceness and wrath of Almighty God" (Revelation 19:15) for just one moment; but you must suffer for all eternity. . . . You will

> know without question that you must wear out long ages, millions and millions of ages, in wrestling and conflicting with this almighty, merciless vengeance. . . . [And] when so many ages have actually been spent by you in this manner, you will know everything you have suffered is but a pinpoint compared to what remains. Your punishment will indeed be infinite.[8]

Sure, there's a lot of chatter in the pseudo-church discounting hell, but there is no intellectually honest way to escape the obvious meaning of the Lord's words on the topic. Words matter. . . and they always mean what they mean. . . especially when they are coming from the Son.

Without question, eternal conscious punishment is the most hated doctrine in the Bible, but it is the indisputably clear teaching of God incarnate. Hell is real. Jesus Christ said so. If you're biblically literate it is no surprise to you that we learn more about hell from the lips of Christ than from any other biblical source.

In a very broad stroke summary, the Son said hell is eternal. It is terrible. It is deserved. And once there, it is inescapable. We must seek to comprehend this reality to the degree our finite capacities will allow. And what's at stake in a deep understanding of the doctrine of hell? Nothing less than a right comprehension of our God, our worship, our sin, and His cross.

---

8 Jonathan Edwards, *Sinners in the Hands of an Angry God*, (New Kensington, PA: Whitaker House, 1997), 56-57.

❖

"... the angels shall come forth, and
take out the wicked from among the
righteous, and will cast them into
the furnace of fire. ..."
Matthew 13:49-50

23

Hell—The Lamb's Presence

"And cast out the worthless slave into the outer darkness. . . ."
Matthew 25:30

Embedded within the words of Jesus Christ regarding hell, in short, we hear that it is a place of darkness, rage, despair, banishment, separation, loneliness, deprivation, loss, suffering, decay, distress, guilt, pressure, affliction, anguish, confinement, contempt, wretchedness, misery, shame, hopelessness, fire, pain, curse, ruin, torment, agony, and horror, etc., etc., etc.!

If Jesus Christ was so painstakingly clear about the reality and nature of hell, it raises the obvious question: Why does your average religious professional never mention any of this? Sadly, we all know why, don't we?

It's interesting that the phrase Jesus used most often (seven times) to describe the sinner in hell is that of "weeping and gnashing of teeth." What is the Lord telling us? In his weeping, doubtless the occupant of hell is utterly self-consumed with his own hopeless plight. This weeping is not about remorse and repentance, however. He is not sorry for his rebellion; he is only sorry for its God-decreed consequence.

No doubt the gnashing of teeth not only connotes the pain of the inhabitant of hell but also his extreme anger. So, who is the object of this ire? While there is certainly an acute self-loathing involved, as well as an ardent hatred for everyone else confined there, principally the rage of the resident of hell is directed at God.

The rebel hated God in this life and hell has not changed that. In fact, hell has deeply intensified that emotion. Hell is not redemptive. It only amplifies man's natural loathing of the biblical God.

There's another kind of rage in hell. That is, God's infinite wrath, anger, and vengeance. The biblical God is omnipresent. He is, by self-description, in hell. David tells us that if he makes his bed in "hell" God is there. The Bible's most frequent description of hell is that of fire. In Scripture, fire is a recurring phenomenon in the manifest presence of God. In His fiery ferocity, God is in hell—terrifyingly so. There are no atheists or agnostics in hell—they all believe!

The prophet tells us that, "The breath of the LORD, [is] like a torrent of brimstone. . ." And regarding God's presence in the punishment of the wicked, the apostle records that the rebel ". . . will be tormented with fire and brimstone in the presence of the holy angels and in the *presence of the Lamb*" (Revelation 14:10).

Sadly, we are all aware that there are many who, without any biblical grounds, simply assert that punishment in hell could not be forever. Such a proposition offends human sensibilities and so there. . . it cannot possibly be what the Scriptures are teaching. Suffice to say, unregenerate human emotions are a poor hermeneutic. The text that ends any legitimate debate on whether hell is, in fact, eternal conscious punishment for those sent there, is Matthew 25:41, 46. Jesus says,

> . . . depart from Me, accused ones, into the eternal fire which has been prepared for the devil and his angels. . . . And these will go away into eternal punishment, but the righteous into eternal life.

You can't run from the same Greek word translated "eternal" being used in the same verse to describe both life and punishment beyond the grave. Jesus could not have been any clearer on this point. Your typical eight-year-old with average comprehension skills understands exactly what the Son is communicating. We all do.

"These shall be punished with
everlasting destruction. . . ."
2 Thessalonians 1:9 (NKJV)

24

Hell—Beyond Human Description

"... and they will be tormented day and night forever and ever."
Revelation 20:10

Granted, eternal conscious punishment is a weighty biblical truth—one that plainly crushes our finite capacities to even begin to comprehend all that it portends. Thoughtful Christians can and do struggle with this truth, but the true believer never dares question the righteousness of God in the face of this doctrine's overwhelming scope.

God is God, and we're not. He does not need or seek our counsel in any aspect of His cosmic administrations, much less His holy verdict against rebellious humanity. With all empathy and humility, I simply ask—what exactly did you expect from the thrice, and yes, fiercely holy I AM WHO I AM Sovereign Creator-God of heaven and earth?

Did you expect a wrath the finite mind could easily accommodate? Did you expect a damnation more in keeping with fallen human sensibilities? Unquestionably, it is one of mankind's gravest miscalculations as God has affirmed through His psalmist, "You thought that I was just like you. . . ."

One of the most common objections to eternal conscious punishment is the fact that our sin, committed in time, is forever punished. 78.69 years of sin is punished everlastingly. The math is a problem for some. There are two fairly obvious reasons that punishment for sin committed in the context of finite time necessarily leads to a never-ending sentence in hell.

First and principally, our sin is against eternal and infinite God. Consequently, the punishment for such offense is inescapably eternal and infinite.

Secondly, and often overlooked, is the fact that the occupant of hell never stops sinning. As a moral creature in premeditated rebellion, proactively hating God with all his being, he never ceases to be guilty before the Creator—forever. His temporal antipathy toward God follows him into eternity. His perpetual sin perpetually fuels the eternality of his hell.

In reaction to Jesus' blunt, graphic, and horrifying description of eternal damnation, many false teachers have sought to simply dispense with the obvious meaning of His words by proposing some variety of universalism or annihilationism. There is only one problem with these types of arguments. They are wholly bereft of any biblical support.

In fact, each, in one way or another, flatly contradicts the words of the Son of God. They are demonstrably heretical. As someone somewhere said, if any of these propositions are true, Jesus Christ was either an incompetent theologian, or He was a liar.

Regarding the ghastly images the Bible uses to describe hell, contemporary American theologian Jim Elliff says that these are, "signposts to something worse." He continues, "What if the true hell can only be experienced, and not described?"[9] In short, the horrors and terrors of hell cannot in any conceivable way be overstated. Hell is ultimately beyond human description.

---

9   Jim Elliff, "My Darkest Night; Hopefully Not Yours," Christian Communicators Worldwide, April 9, 2013, accessed June 6, 2019, http://www.ccwtoday.org/article/my-darkest-night-hopefully-not-yours/#sthash.G2DttBv8.dpuf.

"And if anyone's name was not found written in the book of life, he was thrown into the lake of fire."
Revelation 20:15

25

The Angry Lamb

". . . Terror is on every side."
Jeremiah 6:25

You can't read God's sixty-sixth book and not feel it. The terror that is. Dread and horror fill the pages of God's final book. It's Yahweh's promise to all who have willfully made themselves His enemy.

God says, "Vengeance is Mine, I will repay. . . ." His prophet adds, "The recompense of God will come. . . ." Yes, it is coming. For at the end of the age, John tells us that *all* men *everywhere* will cry out to the mountains and the rocks,

> Fall on us and hide us from the presence of Him who sits on the throne, and from the wrath of the Lamb, for the great day of their wrath has come; who is able to stand?
> (Revelation 6:16-17)

If you've read the sixty-sixth book, you know that no im penitent person will stand in the face of God's omnipotent fury. Indeed, as the apostle writes, they will prefer suicide to standing before the angry Lamb. But death is no escape. It is only the beginning of infinite terror. Lamb-phobia is no exaggerated dread. The angry Lamb is the consummate human horror! And there will never be any escape from His terrifying presence—forever!

So, here's an interesting question arising from the sixty-sixth book: What are the holiest of saints in heaven praying about? Those who were martyred for their faithfulness to the word of God—for what are they praying? Your average church member would never guess. John tells us these holy ones are praying for one thing—vengeance!

> How long O Lord, holy and true, will You refrain from
> judging and avenging our blood on those who dwell
> on the earth?
> (Revelation 6:10)

Every true disciple of Christ knows that with God's final judgment, the wicked will be eternally cast off, ushering in everlasting righteousness for the redeemed in the new heaven and new earth. Yes! As David sings! In all these things, "The righteous man will be glad. . . ." Amen! We will be very, very glad when God unleashes His conclusive fury!

No true believer pretends to be more longsuffering and compassionate than God. We, like our Father, have a taste for this—for the glory of God in His spent wrath. Yes, we will eagerly join the multitudes of heaven in singing, "Hallelujah! Hallelujah!" as God "avenges the blood of His bond-servants" and deals "out retribution to those who do not know God. . . and do not obey the gospel. . . ." (Revelation 19:1-3, 2 Thessalonians 1:8).

Parenthetically, vengeance is not our job. This is God's right alone. The Bible makes this clear for every follower of Jesus Christ. God says to every professed Christian. . .

> Never take your own vengeance, but leave room for
> the wrath of God, 'Vengeance is Mine, I will repay,'
> says the Lord.
> (Romans 12:19)

Vengeance is not ours. It's God's. He actually says, it is "Mine." So, we're to leave it alone. He tells us He is coming quickly and will be bringing all of His wrath with Him. No one gets away with anything. . . no one. All moral accounts will be perfectly settled.

❖

"For the day of vengeance was
in My heart. . . ."
Isaiah 63:4

26

The Atrophied Church

*"Those whom I love, I reprove
and discipline; be zealous
therefore, and repent."*
Revelation 3:19

In the early chapters of Revelation, God begins with His professing church. It's what the Lord told us through Peter's pen which is really the perfect entree into the sixty-sixth book for both the believer and the unbeliever. . .

> For it is time for judgment to begin with the household of God; and if it begins with us first, what will be the outcome for those who do not obey the gospel of God? And if it is with difficulty that the righteous is saved, what will become of the godless man and the sinner?
> (1 Peter 4:17-18)

So yes, God begins His final book with those called by His name. He directly addresses seven churches. Five are, to say the least, falling short. Ephesus had left its "first love." Pergamum and Thyatira were tolerating sin. Sardis was, in the Lord's words, "dead," in need of repentance—for there were but a "few" true believers. And last, was the infamous church of Laodicea—the only church to which God has nothing good to say.

Laodicea is an atrophied church. A Laodicean-type church today still bears the name Christian, but it doesn't really believe much of anything anymore. It still uses biblical words and concepts, but it is mostly religious routine. It still meets on Sunday, but most members don't honestly remember why.

The church in Laodicea professed to be rich, and in fact its members were, in a material sense, but spiritually, God said they were wretched, miserable, poor, blind, and naked. Christ says. . .

> I know your deeds, that you are neither cold nor hot. I could wish you were cold or hot. So then, because you are lukewarm, and neither cold nor hot, I will vomit you out of My mouth.
> (Revelation 3:15-16, NKJV)

Could the Lord be any clearer? The lukewarm church member makes Him sick! He or she makes God gag! Sadly, Laodicea is a picture of the pervasive reality in the modern era. Many professing Christians are so utterly immersed in simply doing church for the sake of doing it, that they are oblivious to the fact that Christ will not receive their muddled, contrived, and wholly superficial worship.

Many such churchgoers profess some sort of belief in Christ, but do not truly know Him or love Him. Many belong to a purported church and attend semi-regularly but are not genuinely serious about obeying the Lord in the world. This can be nothing but a stench in the nostrils of Yahweh.

The sixty-sixth book is unambiguous. Jesus Christ is coming. Judgment is coming. Wrath is coming. Vengeance is coming. The second death is coming. This will happen. "Every eye" will see it. And we will delight in His vengeance as do the saints in heaven, or we will be swept into hell by it. It's our call, for God has provided a remedy for any and all who would repent and believe. . . just turn the page.

*"Woe, woe, woe, to those who
dwell on the earth. . . ."*
Revelation 8:13

27

The Bottom-Line Question

"For Christ also died for sins. . . in order that He might bring us to God. . . ."
1 Peter 3:18

We won't come to God—without God. We have no desire for God—apart from God. We don't want God. Not really. If we are to ever come to God, we must be brought to God by God. Apart from our Creator invading our lives, rescuing us from ourselves, and bringing us to Himself, we will forever remain His enemy. It's what God says. It's who we are. It's the core truth of Peter's words noted above.

Some readers may protest. Some of you may believe that you sought God on your own. Some of you feel like you took the initiative. You may have made a decision for Christ. You may have asked Jesus into your heart—yes, that incantation-like prayer. You may have been baptized. You might regularly attend the worship services of a respectable denomination. But I'm talking about the root issue for every human being.

I'm asking you to be brutally honest with yourself—to take a long, hard look in the mirror. This matters. It matters a lot. It matters forever. This is likely the most important question you've ever been asked to consider. I caution you—don't just parrot what you know you're supposed to say. Maybe for the first time in your life, think deeply about this and be truthful.

Here's the bottom-line question—Aren't many professed Christians truly more interested in someone, or something, or some accomplishment, or some recognition, or some acquisition, or some security, or some comfort, or some experience, or some worldly pleasure than they are in God? Isn't this who multitudes of so-called Christians really are, despite all the church-going and Jesus-talk? I pray this is not true of you, but in light of the stakes, as narrated in this book, isn't it worth some serious reflection?

It's a shocking reality! It truly is hard to believe that humanity is genuinely more fascinated with some created thing or some temporal experience than with its Creator. This is stunningly and universally true. God's apostle affirms it as is noted earlier in the book. He bluntly writes, ". . . There is none who seek for God." Yes, that's each and every one of us.

Considering our chosen and premeditated alienation from God, we desperately need Someone to bring us to Him. To reconcile us to God. To resolve the wrath, vengeance, recompense, and terror problem that we all have.

There is only one Someone who can—Jesus Christ. Again, we're talking about the biblical Jesus, not the pseudo-christs preached in many so-called churches every Sunday morning. The Bible is soberingly clear—God the Son and God the Spirit must bring us to God the Father, because we will not otherwise seek, nor come to Him.

Scripture is alarmingly blunt: left to our own devices, we would all land in hell. This is who we are. This is biblical truth. We are damned without His overture, without His coming, without Him atoning for our sins, without Him regenerating us, without God bringing us to God!

*"By this will we have been sanctified
through the offering of the
body of Jesus Christ. . . ."*
Hebrews 10:10

28

Stunned, Staggered, Breathless Awe!

"For a child will be born to us. . . . And His name will be called Wonderful, Counselor, . . . Mighty God, Eternal Father, Prince of Peace."
Isaiah 9:6

And there He is. He's in that manger. Mighty God is in a manger. Unsought. Unsolicited. Uninvited. Unwanted. Mankind's Savior conceived by the Spirit and born to two nobodies in a nowhere place. Yahweh in a body. Emmanuel, God with us.

Yes, it is breathtaking. Stunningly so for anyone who thinks about it for more than thirty seconds. You're right—this does change everything forever. He obviously matters more than anyone or anything else possibly ever could. To paraphrase nineteenth-century English preacher Charles Spurgeon, this Son of Mary and Joseph is—Infinite, yet infant. . . eternal, yet born. . . almighty, yet suckled. . . .upholding a universe, yet lying in a manger.

English theologian J. I. Packer sums it up perfectly, as he writes, ". . . the more you think about it, the more staggering it is." If you're not genuinely staggered, you've not really understood it. If you're not stunned, you've not truly believed it.

The Alpha and Omega Creator-God is in a manger! The galaxy-breathing-galaxy-sustaining God is in a manger! I AM-El-Shaddai God is in a manger! Let the whole created order, and every thinking, sentient being in it, stand in stunned, staggered, breathless awe! God has come to save His people from their self-absorbed selves!

If you've read this far in this book, you know we all have an insurmountable problem with an exceedingly dangerous God—an urgent problem none of us can solve. The first three verses of Ephesians 2 tell us we are spiritually dead, captive to Satan, and, by nature. . . children of wrath.

In response to our dilemma, the very next verse begins with two of the most beautiful words ever recorded. The apostle tells us that yes, we're dead, yes, we're captive, yes, we're damned. Then he writes, "But God. . ." But God what? "But God, being rich in mercy, because of the great love with which He loved us. . . made us alive together with Christ. . . ." God is our remedy. God came that He might bring us to God. God made a way. He didn't staff this out. In love, He came to make the dead alive—to set the captive free—to expunge the wrath we deserve. He's in that manger because He is going to the Cross to save a people for the glory of His name!

Men of their own free, depraved, rebellious wills murdered the Son of God. God of His own free, gracious, loving will redeemed His people. God the Father did not spare His own Son but delivered Him up. God the Son laid His life down of His own initiative.

This was God's idea. The crucifixion of God was a God-ordained, God-decreed, God-planned, God-initiated event. With resolute and unwavering premeditation, Jesus Christ went to the cross. He told Pilate, "For this I have been born."

*". . . From you One will go forth for Me
to be ruler in Israel. His goings forth
are from long ago, from
the days of eternity."*
Micah 5:2

29

"Mary!"

---

*"He is not here, for He has
risen, just as He said. . . ."*
Matthew 28:6

There are a lot of pseudo-intellectuals who deny the physical resurrection of Jesus Christ. I will not waste any time refuting them. This is simply a matter of believing what the Bible clearly asserts. The Scriptures affirm that Jesus appeared no fewer than ten times over a period of forty days to more than five hundred people.

Real Christians don't believe Christ is risen merely because of the objective physical evidences. Certainly, we rejoice in the biblical testimony as well as in the historical proofs and logical inferences that verify His resurrection; but that is not finally why we believe. We believe because of one undeniable and irrefutable fact. It's the very same reason Mary Magdalene believed.

It was early Sunday morning and Mary Magdalene was at Jesus' tomb. She was weeping for no good reason. She had much love, but no faith. This is one of the striking things about the resurrection of Christ—none of His followers expected it. They were the first skeptics. He'd told them numerous times that He would rise, but not one of them believed Him.

Mary was crying, but Jesus had given her His promise that He would rise and yes. . . there He is. He asked her why she was weeping but she did not recognize Him. So how does Mary ultimately come to believe that Jesus had risen? Jesus said to her, "Mary!" Immediately, she knew it was her Savior! No one could speak her name like He could—full of God-sized love and intimacy!

The good Shepherd calls one of His sheep by name, and she knows! That's how every true believer knows. Genuine Christianity is never only about right doctrine. Satan believes the facts. It's always about a breathtaking God-encounter resulting in a life-changing, eternity-altering metamorphosis. It's always the "born-again" work of the Holy Spirit—the blooming of the sacred romance.

Biblical Christianity is not merely religion. It is relationship. Remember what Jesus told the religious leaders? He said, "You do not believe because you are not of My sheep." A lot of people who call themselves Christians don't like it when God talks that way; but that's how He talks. The Lord said, "I am the good shepherd and I know My own and My own know Me. . . .[and] My sheep hear My voice, and I know them, and they follow Me." Mary immediately recognizes the voice of her Shepherd, the One who had laid "down His life for the sheep." Jesus said. . .

> For this reason, the Father loves Me, because I lay down My life that I may take it up again. No one has taken it away from Me, but I lay it down on My own initiative. . . . and I give eternal life to [the sheep], and they shall never perish; and no one shall snatch them out of My hand.
> (John 10:17-18, 28-29)

*"He who was delivered up because
of our transgressions and was raised
because of our justification."*
Romans 4:25

30

Do You Really Believe?

---

*"... but these have been written
that you may believe that Jesus
is the Christ, the Son of God;
and that believing you may
have life in His name."*
John 20:31

Google tells me there are 2.2 billion people who profess to believe that God is in that manger in Bethlehem and on that cross in Jerusalem. At Christmas and Easter, multitudes of people pour into churches, many of whom attend only on those occasions.

They profess to believe, but you can tell many really don't. You can tell because their so-called "before Jesus life" is mostly identical to their so-called "after Jesus life" except, as Francis Chan said somewhere, with a determined effort to "cuss less."

You can tell that many don't truly believe because there is no life-altering awe, wonder, joy, worship, and obedience pouring out of their lives. If one really believes that God is in that manger and on that cross, there is not one part of the life that will not change. You simply can't genuinely believe the Christmas-Easter story in a lifestyle vacuum.

If you really believe it. . . it will be way more than a semi-irregular-church-attendance kind of thing. In fact, it won't be religious at all. It will be an intensely personal thing. You will have met your Creator. You will have begun to know, love, trust, and obey Him. The relationship is real. It is intimate. It is dynamic.

As every born-again Christian can testify, loving Christ is the only life worth living. It always manifests as a radical outward response to God's radical invasion of our lives. Eugene Peterson perfectly captures what this looks like in the true believer's life as he writes, ". . . Take your everyday, ordinary life—your sleeping, eating, going to work, and walking around life—and place it before God as an offering."[10]

A radically transformed life is the obvious and compelling reality of every born-again believer caught up in the Christmas and Easter stories. Nothing was ever the same for Mary, Joseph, the shepherds, and the magi at Christ's birth. And of course, nothing was ever the same for Mary Magdalene, Peter, James, John, and the rest at His resurrection.

Sure, Satan and his minions believe. They believe so much that they tremble. The test is never in merely believing the facts. The test is always in loving the Christ!

So, do you really believe? Have you genuinely come to Jesus Christ and thus escaped the righteous wrath, vengeance, recompense, and terror of a justly incensed and dangerous God? God's apostle tells us how we can know. . .

> And by this we know that we have come to know Him if we keep His commandments. The one who says, "I have come to know Him," and does not keep His commandments, is a liar, and the truth is not in him; but whoever keeps His word, in him the love of God has truly been perfected. By this we know that we are in Him: the one who says he abides in Him ought himself to walk in the same manner as He walked.
> (1 John 2:3-6)

---

10   Romans 12:1, The Message Bible.

*". . . how shall we escape if we neglect
so great a salvation?"*
Hebrews 2:3

31

A Thrilling Fear

". . . I know that it will be well
for those who fear God, who
fear Him openly."
Ecclesiastes 8:12

The fear of God is the most beautiful, powerful, meaningful, fulfilling, and yes, exuberant place to live. If you call yourself a Christian and don't know that—you're doing it wrong.

You've not yet learned the indispensable lesson of this life—to tremble before your Creator with complete delight in abandoned worship. A deep peace and enduring joy arise through the sanctifying process of yielding to God as He crushes the hubris and self-importance out of our lives. This happens only as we learn God correctly, coming to fear Him as He has commanded. Truly, this is the most devastatingly humbling yet exquisitely enlightening epiphany a human being can experience.

For indeed, to genuinely fear the biblical God is to fear nothing else. To fear the biblical God is to be progressively liberated from every form of anxiety and slavery. To fear the biblical God is to find the breathtaking purpose for which your soul and mind were created—namely, ever-intensifying, awed intimacy with your Maker.

The proper fear of God—this stunned wonder and captivated reverence—fully animates the human spirit and intellect. To walk in perpetual amazement of Yahweh is to be truly alive! To learn to consciously abide in the never-ending, ever-increasing wonderment of Jesus Christ, is to fully live.

We cannot settle for merely attending religious services and knowing biblical facts. We must encounter and know our Creator-Redeemer God in all His fullness. It is no matter that this pursuit starts in time and will ultimately consume a billion eternities—for it will be a billion eternities flawlessly spent! As theologian John Piper writes. . .

"For most of us, fear is something we want to get rid of, not get more of. If that's true of the fear of the Lord, then there is something wrong with our hearts or something wrong with our understanding of this fear. Have you ever gathered up the spectacular promises made to those who fear God? They are so wonderful that you would think fearing God must be the most thrilling thing in the world—which it is."[11]

Here are God's promises to those who fear Him:

- Psalm 25:14—"The secret of the Lord is for those who fear Him, and He will make them know His covenant."
- Psalm 33:18—"Behold, the eye of the Lord is on those who fear Him. . . ."
- Psalm 34:7—"The angel of the Lord encamps around those who fear Him, and rescues them."
- Psalm 34:9—"O fear the Lord, you His saints; For to those who fear Him, there is no want."
- Psalm 103:13—". . . the Lord has compassion on those who fear Him."
- Psalm 103:17—"But the lovingkindness of the Lord is from everlasting to everlasting on those who fear Him. . . ."
- Psalm 147:11—"The Lord favors those who fear Him. . . ."
- Proverbs 19:23—"The fear of the Lord leads to life. . . ."

Dangerous God says for those who fear Me there is My secret, My watch-care, My rescue, My provision, My compassion, My everlasting lovingkindness, My favor, and My forever life! And yes! Yes, as the psalmist sings, "There is forgiveness with You, that You may be feared" (Psalm 130:4).

11   John Piper, *A Godward Life* (Sisters, OR: Multnomah Publishers, 1997), 246.

"... work out you own salvation with
fear and trembling; for it is God who
is at work in you, both to will and to
work for His good pleasure."
Philippians 2:12-13

About the Author

At the age of forty-two, Jim left a twenty-year business career to answer God's call to preach. From early 2004 to mid 2022, he and his wife, Karen, lived in Milan, Italy, where Jim was the pastor of the International Church of Milan, a non-denominational, Bible-teaching church ministering to internationals from around the globe. Jim is now an elder at Grace Baptist Church in Scott, Arkansas, and he is a co-founder of Dangerous God Ministries. Jim holds a Master of Divinity degree from Midwestern Baptist Theological Seminary (SBC). In addition to *Dangerous God*, Jim has published two other books: *Uncareful Lives*, and *Everything Says Glory*—all of which are available on Amazon.

Learn more about Jim Albright at
http://www.greatwriting.org/author-albright
You can find Jim's sermons at
https://pastorjimpodcast.podbean.com/

www.dangerousgod.com

We proclaim the terrifyingly good news of a Dangerous God so as to fully behold both the severity of His holiness and the kindness of His grace. Contact us if you wish to arrange a seminar at your church. Use the contact form to reach us from our website.

Everything says Glory
978-0996516884
Trade Paperback, 200pp

Cutting-edge science has revealed that Darwinian evolutionary theory is dead. The postmortem is complete. Yes, of course, the God hypothesis is indispensable! Christian, we have the data! God is calling you to wield it! Read, Learn, Worship, Tell!

In seven articulately written chapters, Jim Albright persuasively pinpoints and exposes the pseudo-scientific tenets of macro-evolutionary thinking. Replete with quotations from scientists across many disciplines, this is a book that every Christian should own. Missionary Keith Jones is right, "The best part of this book is that it will provoke you to a whole new level of worship!"

Dangerous God
9781734345278
Trade Paperback, 178pp

. . . Sure, you have some concept of a supreme being—but, is your god-notion, God? The one true God? The biblical God? The God who is?

To anyone who has ears to hear, I simply say that it's time to open the Book and truly behold the dreadful holiness and terrifying awe of I AM. Certainly, it is long past time in this era of low-resolution preaching, denominational banality, and pervasive biblical illiteracy. For indeed, the Bible is unmistakably clear. . .

"It is a terrifying thing to fall into the hands of the living God."

(Hebrews 10:31)

Dangerous God Study Guide
978-1735949192
Trade Paperback, 96pp

God is probably not who you think He is. . .

How can you be sure? Why does it matter?

Do you know the God of fierce wrath and horrifying vengeance? Is this the God you worship?

Is it possible that much of the modern church has settled for a domesticated, pseudo-Christ?

Do you understand that God has revealed that He is dreadfully provoked? Do you know why?

Uncareful Lives: Walking Where Feet May Fail
978-1620205303
Trade Paperback, 160pp

"Come!"—Jesus Christ, Matthew 14:29

It's God's invitation into the uncareful life – a life of courageous faith. Come, and see how awesome He is! Come, and see who you're supposed to be!

Christian, our God is God! You can do all He says because He will do all He says. He is your license to live your faith as big as you dare. He is your liberty to embrace a life big with God-pleasing, God-encountering faith. He is your freedom to wholeheartedly engage in fully-persuaded, never-look-back, no-risk-is-too-great, glad-fearless-joy obedience! Come on, you know you want to! You know you've always wanted to—ever since you heard Him whisper, "Follow Me." What are you waiting for? Whatever it is, it's a lie.

www.ingramcontent.com/pod-product-compliance
Lightning Source LLC
Chambersburg PA
CBHW071439130726
47997CB00006B/2147